McGRAW-HILL READING

Authors

James Flood

Jan E. Hasbrouck

James V. Hoffman

Diane Lapp

Angela Shelf Medearis

Scott Paris

Steven Stahl

Josefina Villamil Tinajero

Karen D. Wood

 **McGraw-Hill
School Division**

New York   Farmington

Consulting Authors

Barbara Coulter, Frankie Dungan, Joseph B. Rubin,
Carl B. Smith, Shirley Wright

McGraw-Hill **School Division**
A Division of The **McGraw·Hill** *Companies*

McGraw-Hill School Division
Two Penn Plaza
New York, New York 10121

Printed in the United States of America

ISBN 0-02-188297-5/1, Vol. 1

2 3 4 5 6 7 8 9 043/071 04 03 02 01 00

Volume 1

Cat Club

written by Amy Jo

illustrated by Carol Nicklaus

Pat Cat has hats with dots.

Sam Cat has jam and hams.

Pam Cat has black bats.

Nan Cat has yams in pans.

The cats run to Max Cat.

The cats have fun, fun, fun!

The End

Cats, Cats, Cats

written by Amy Jo

illustrated by Mike Maydak

This cat is tan and black.

It can run and swim well.

This cat runs fast, fast, fast.

It hunts in the hot, hot sun.

This big, big cat is king.

It can yell and yell and yell.

My cat can nap and nap with me!

The End

Back to Camp

written by Amy Jo

illustrated by Luisa D'Augusta

Pat and Nick set the clock.

Click, click, tick, tock, tick.

Pat and Nick pack and pack.

Pat and Nick pack tan pants.

Pat and Nick add black socks.

Dad stacks bags in the van.

Pat is at camp at last.

Nick is at camp at last.

CAMP

28

The End

Pick Up Pup!

written by Amy Jo

illustrated by Jean Hirashima

PUPS

Tan pup is glad, Jack.

It jumps and nips.

Fat pup runs and jumps, Fran.

Let's pick fat pup.

Big pup is fun!

It licks and licks.

Let's get this pack of pups!

The End

Pig's Trip

written by Bonnie Jill Lee

illustrated by Vicki Learner

The clock helps Pig get up.

Pig packs for his trip.

Pig packs his map and mitt.

Pig packs his gift and tricks.

Pig gets on the jet at last.

Kim picks him up at six.

Kim gives Pig a big, big kiss!

The End

Rick's Desk

written by Bonnie Jill Lee

illustrated by Lauren Cryan

Rick's desk is a mess.

Rick can fix his desk quick!

Rick fits ten pens in a box.

Rick gets clips in the cup.

Rick licks six stamps.

Rick scrubs his desk well.

Rick's desk is not a mess.

Rick can have fun.

52

Max Gets His Wish

written by Bonnie Jill Lee

illustrated by Ken Spengler

This is Max's ship.

Max will sit in the sun.

55

Max will jog on a deck.

Max will not have a bath!

This is Max's rod.

Max will wish for a big fish.

That's Max and his fish!
Max gets his wish!

The End

CAT AND HIS PALS

written by Bonnie Jill Lee

illustrated by Richard Kolding

Three bees got in a cab.

Three bees wish to see Cat.

Three bees will give Cat a gift.

Duck and Pig see the three bees.

Three bees dash on Cat's path.

Cat sees his pals and is glad.

Cat and his pals sit and sip!

The End

Pup and Bug

written by Gary Apple

illustrated by Bernard Adnet

Pup sees Big Bug.

Big Bug sees Pup!

Big Bug runs on the big, red rug.

Pup runs on the big, red rug.

Is Big Bug on the mat?

Big Bug is in the tub!

Is Big Bug in the dish?
Big Bug is on the bun!

Is Big Bug in the mug?
Big Bug is on the duck!

Pup can see Big Bug.

Big Bug is on the fat cat!

Pup jumps on top of the cat.

Big Bug is in luck!

The End

Bud Has Six Pups

written by Gary Apple

illustrated by Diana Magnuson

Bud has six small pups.

That is a lot of pups!

Bud's pups get up at ten.

Bud's six pups jump and jump.

Bud sees the sun!
Bud and his six pups go out.

Bud gives his pups a ride.
Bud and his pups have fun
in the sun.

Bud's pups jump and run.

Bud's pups dig and hop in the mud!

Bud gives his pups a bath in the tub.
Bud gets wet!

Bud tucks his six pups in six
dog beds.

He tucks his pups in—tuck,
tuck, tuck, tuck, tuck, and tuck!

The End

Dot in Pop's Shop

written by Gary Apple

illustrated by Flora Jew

Dot is a big, fat cat.

He sits in Pop's shop.

Dot jumps up on this big, black pot.

He slips on top.

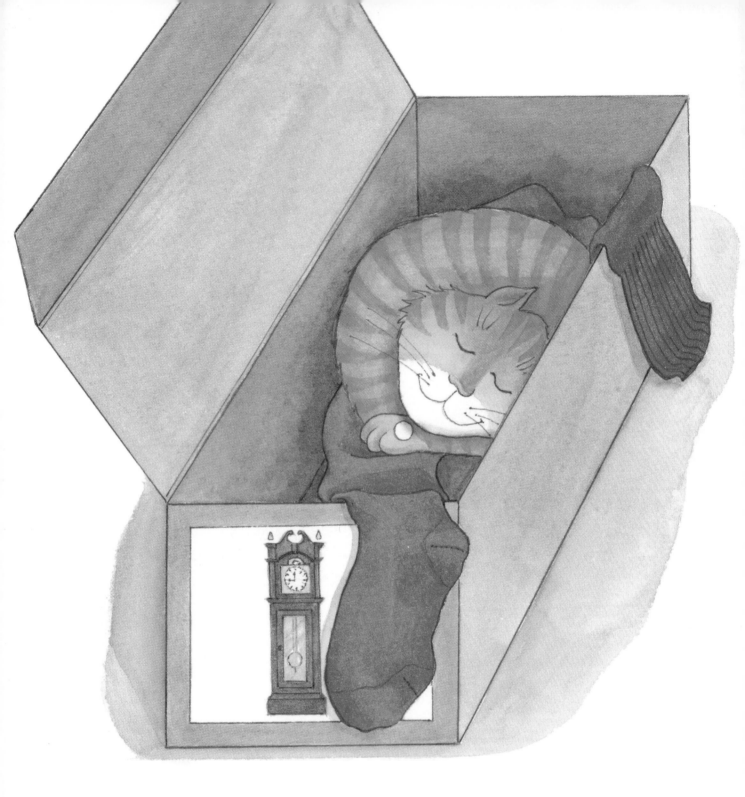

Dot naps on this red sock.

The red sock is in this

big clock box.

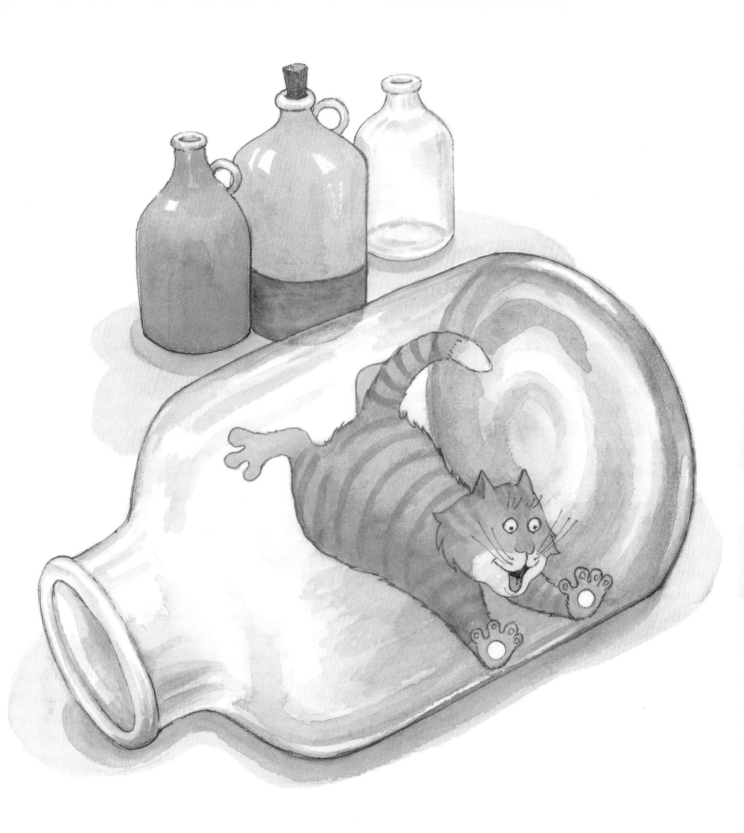

Dot can run in that big jug.
He gets in and runs and runs.

Dot hops on Pop's clock.

He rocks and rocks.

Dot runs to the dolls.

Dot has fun with this doll's wigs.

Dot has lots of fun in Pop's shop.

It is fun to be Pop's cat, Dot.

The End

BOB BUG

written by Gary Apple

illustrated by Sharron O'Neil

Bob Bug felt sad.

"I am small," sobbed Bob Bug.

Bob Bug met his pal Dot Duck.
"Dot Duck is big!" sobbed Bob Bug.

"Yes, yes, yes," Dot Duck quacked.
"Big is fun, fun, fun!"

Bob Bug met his pal Don Dog.
"Don Dog is big!" sobbed Bob Bug.

"Yes, yes, yes," Don Dog said.
"Big is fun, fun, fun!"

Sad Bob Bug sat and sobbed.
Then Buglet met Bob Bug.

"You are big, Bob Bug!" said Buglet.

"Yes!" said Bob Bug. "To you I am big, big, big!"

The End

WET PETS

written by Robyn Pickering
illustrated by Jeffery Severn

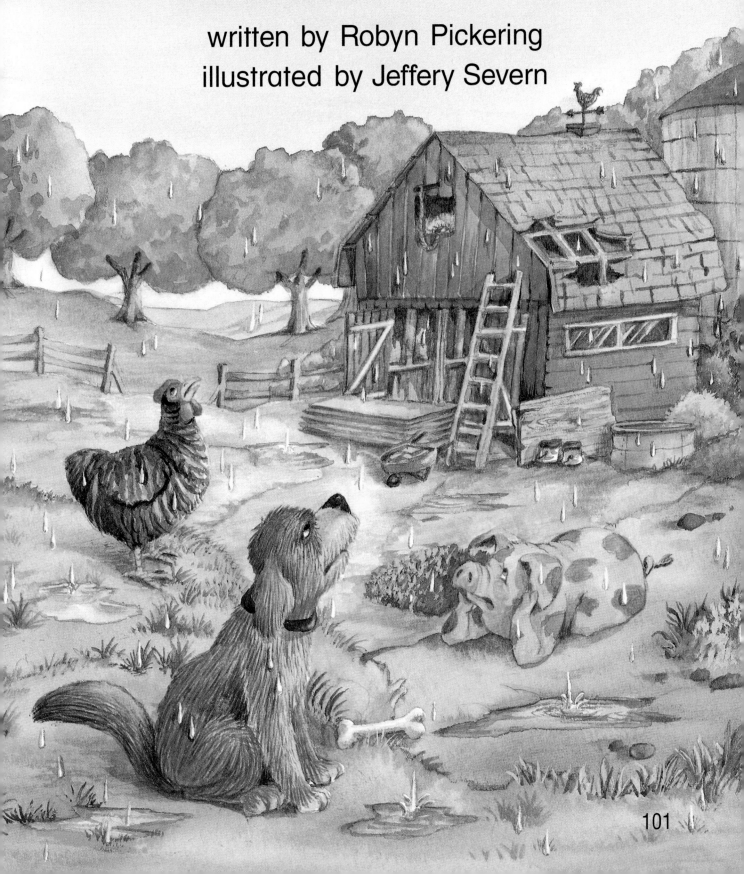

Hen pecks in the wet wet pen.
It is not fun to be wet.

Pig naps in the wet wet mud.
It is not fun to be wet.

Dog sits in the wet wet grass.
It is not fun to be wet.

Ben sees his wet pets.

He wants to help Hen, Pig, and Dog.

Ben lets them in the red shed.
It is not wet!

Hen pecks.

It is not wet in the shed.

Dog and Pig sit.

It is not wet in the shed, not yet.

The End

In the Hot Sun

written by Robyn Pickering

illustrated by Kathi Ember

I get up and look out.

It is wet and I am sad.

This is me in a red hat in the
hot sun. It is not wet and
I am not sad.

That is Mom's big tan dog, Seth.
He is with me.

That is Dad's fat cat, Socks.
She is with Seth and me.

Look! It is not wet out.

Seth and Socks run out with me.

The End

Let's Go See Bugs

written by Michael Lee
illustrated by Andrea Champlin

"Look!" yelled Jill. "A fat red bug on my math book!"

118

Miss Kim took Jill's math book, and put the fat red bug in the big jar.

Jill sat and looked at it.
It had thin red wings.

"Can bugs be good pets?"
said Nell.

"Not as good as dogs,"
said Rick.

"Not as good as cats.
Not as good as frogs and fish."

122

"As good as pigs?" yelled Jan.

"We can go see lots of bugs," said Miss Kim.

123

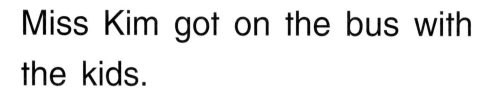

Miss Kim got on the bus with the kids.

"To see bugs will be fun!" yelled Jill.

124

The End

Bee and Duck

written by Cynthia Rothman

illustrated by Jo-Ellen Bosson

Duck is so sick.

Duck has lost his quack.

"I wish to help Duck," said Dog.
Dog will pack his sack and
then see Duck.

"I wish to help Duck," said Frog. Frog will dash and get cash and then see Duck.

"I wish to help Duck," said Cat.
Cat will look in her shop and
then see Duck.

Duck is still so sick.
Duck sits on a rock but
can not quack.

Buzz Buzz.

Bee wants to see Duck.

Duck runs and lands in a bath!

Quack! Quack!

Duck has his quack back.

The End

BANG, THUMP, PING!

written by Maryann Dobeck

illustrated by Laura Huliska Beith

Skunk napped.
BANG! BANG! BANG!
"What is that?" Skunk asked.

Skunk looked.

He went sniff, sniff, sniff.

But Skunk did not see the thing
that went Bang, Bang, Bang.

Skunk went back to his nap.

THUMP! THUMP! THUMP!

PING! PING! PING!

"What is that?" Skunk yelled.

Skunk looked.

He went sniff, sniff, sniff.

But Skunk did not see the thing
that went Thump and Ping.

BANG! BANG! BANG!
THUMP! THUMP! THUMP!
PING! PING! PING!

Skunk could not stand it.
Skunk did not see the thing that
went Bang, Thump, and Ping.
Then Skunk did see a tall flag.

"Look at that band!" yelled Skunk.
"It's the best band in the land."

The End

I Would if I Could

written by Maryann Dobeck

illustrated by John Carrozza

Fox saw Frog splash in a pond.
"Splash, splash," Frog called.

"A fox can't splash," yelled Fox.
And Fox ran off.

Fox saw Bat nap on a branch.

"Nap with me," Bat called.

"Hmmm, I wish I could," yelled Fox.
And off Fox ran.

Fox saw Bee buzz.

"Buzz, buzz," called Bee.

"A fox can't buzz," yelled Fox.
And Fox ran off.

Fox saw Duck flap and quack.
"Flap and quack with me," called Duck.

"Hmmm, I wish I could," yelled Fox.
And off ran Fox.

Small cubs ran past.

The small cubs ran fast, fast, fast!

Glen blasted his brass trumpet.

Brad drummed his big drum.

Miss Hop clanged a gong.

Miss Hop's class clapped.

Then, Brad and Glen did tricks.

Brad and Glen did twin handstands.

All the kids in the class clapped.

Brad and Glen did twin flips.

Brad and Glen went flip, flop,
flip, flop.

All the kids in the class clapped.

Brad held still. Glen trusted Brad.

Glen jumped and flipped. Plop!

Glen landed on top of Brad.

Brad grabbed Glen's legs.

Then, Glen flung himself down.

Glen dropped and the kids gasped.

Glen did a triple twist.

What a stunt!

Kids clapped and clapped.
Glen and Brad did it.
Miss Hop's class was fun.

The End

Jill and Cliff's Pumpkins

written by Anne Miranda

illustrated by Andrea Champlin

This is Jill and Cliff's land.

Jill and Cliff dig it up.

Jill and Cliff crush any big

clumps with picks.

What will Jill and Cliff grow?

Pumpkins!

Jill and Cliff get six new pumpkin plants.

Jill digs six small pits.

Cliff plants all six plants.

Cliff prints tags.

Jill twists sticks next to all
six pumpkin plants.

Cliff sticks six tags on
six sticks.

Jill and Cliff are all set.

Jill gets an old milk bottle and fills it to the brim. Then Cliff trickles drops on all six plants.

Jill and Cliff's pumpkin plants are still small. Will pumpkins grow from them?

Yes! Jill and Cliff's pumpkin
plants get big.

Jill and Cliff tend the plants
until fall.

In the fall, Jill and Cliff have
a big, big crop.
Jill and Cliff pick lots and lots
of plump pumpkins.

The End

Chet Chick

written by Anne Miranda

illustrated by Winky Adam

Chet Chick was brand new.
Chet was just an inch tall.
Chet sat in his nest on a
big branch. Chet looked up.
"What is that?" gasped Chet.

"Think, Chet," said the thing.

Chet checked and rubbed his chin.
"Mom?" asked Chet.

"Yes, Chet," winked Mom Chick.

Chet looked at a big thing.

"What is that?" gasped Chet.

"Think, Chet," said Mom Chick.

Chet checked and rubbed his chin.

"Lunch?" asked Chet.

"Yes, it is lunch," winked Mom Chick.

"Thanks," said Chet.
Chet munched his lunch.

Chet got big.

"When will I flap my wings?"
asked Chet.

"Think Chet," said Mom Chick.

Chet checked and rubbed his chin.
"I think I can flap."

"Yes, Chet. I think you can,"
winked Mom Chick.

Chet jumped off his branch.
Chet flapped his wings.

"I think I can!" yelled Chet.
Chet flapped and flapped.

"My Chet is such a champ,"
said Mom Chick.

"Thanks, Mom!" winked Chet.

The End

Lunch Kit

written by Anne Miranda

illustrated by Kathi Ember

Chad sat in his tree. Kit Cat
jumped up on the tree trunk.

"What will we get for lunch?"
asked Kit.

Chad had a blank look.

"Lunch?" asked Chad.

"Yes, lunch," said Kit.
"It is the tenth, isn't it?"

Chad checked.
"Look! Ten at lunch!
Ten at lunch! What will we do?"

"Help, Kit! We must cook lunch,
ten lunches," said Chad.
Chad handed Kit eggs, milk, ham,
and a whisk. Chad handed Kit
a flat pan.

"Whip quick, Kit!" said Kit to himself.
So Kit whipped up milk and eggs
in the pan and cooked them.

Next, Kit added ham chunks on top.
Then Kit flipped it from the pan
to a dish.

Chad chopped nuts and apples
at his sink.
Chad mixed in this and that.
Then Chad fixed the pink drink.

Chad and Kit cooked a good lunch.
The lunch looked good, and it
smelled good.

Just then, Chad's bell rang.
"Let them in," said Kit with a wink.
The lunch bunch sat and had the
best lunch yet, thanks to Kit Cat.

The End

Jake's Rake

written by Anne Miranda
illustrated by Angela Adams

Jake took his rake and went out back.

Jane took six big trash bags.

Jake raked up, and Jane stuffed bags.

"Make no mistake, I hate raking,"
huffed Jake.

"Make a game of it," Jane winked.

"I hate games," Jake hissed.

"Want to trade?" asked Jane.

"I hate stuffing bags," huffed Jake.

"Well then rake," said Jane.
Jake raked.

Then Jake yelled and waved
his hands. A thing wiggled.
"What is it?" asked Jake.

"What shape was it?" asked Jane.

"I did not see it," yelled Jake.

Jane was brave. Jane looked.
The thing wiggled. Jake jumped back.
"Save me!"

"It has scales. I think it is a snake," said Jane.

"Let's chase it," yelled Jake.

"No, it is a nest of little snakes," said Jane. "We can save them."

Jake gazed at the little snakes.
"I will save them. Can we make
up names for them?" asked Jake.

Jake and Jane made a tag.

SAVE JAKE'S SNAKES!
NO RAKING THIS SPOT!

Jake gave Jane big hugs.
"Raking is fun."

The End

Kate's Cake

written by Anne Miranda

illustrated by Matt Straub

Kate's pals sat under branches
in the shade.

"Where is Kate's Cake?" asked
Dave Dog.

Kit Cat, Chet Chimp, and Pat Pig
did not know.

Why didn't Kit, Chet, and Pat make
Kate's cake? Dave did not know.
But, Dave went shopping!

Dave got pots and pans. Dave
mixed milk, eggs, and cake mix.
Dave baked Kate's cake.
Dave set Kate's cake on a
big glass plate.

Dave made Kate's cake the same
shape as a big snake.
Dave made fake scales.
Dave scribbled Kate's name.
Dave will take Kate's cake.

"Where is Kate?" asked Dave.

Kit, Chet, and Pat did not know.
Kate was late. Kit, Chet, and Pat
gazed at Kate's snake cake.

"Kate will hate that snake cake," giggled Kit.

"Kate will hate that snake cake," giggled Pat

"Kate will hate that snake cake," giggled Chet.

Kate came at last. Dave gave
Kate his cake.

"Dave, what a cake!" hissed Kate.
And Kate ate the cake in one
big snake gulp.

The End

Word List

CAT CLUB	Decodable Words		High-Frequency Words
	and	jam	has
	bats	Max	have
	black	Nan	the
	cat	Pam	to
	cats	pans	with
	dots	Pat	
	fun	run	
	hams	Sam	
	hats	yams	
	in		

CATS, CATS, CATS	Decodable Words		High-Frequency Words
	big	nap	is
	can	runs	me
	fast	sun	my
	hot	swim	this
	hunts	tan	
	it	well	
	king	yell	

BACK TO CAMP	Decodable Words	
	add	pack
	at	pants
	bags	set
	camp	socks
	click	stacks
	clock	tick
	dad	tock
	last	van
	Nick	

The word list shows where each word first appears.

PICK UP PUP!	Decodable Words		High-Frequency Word
	fat	let's	of
	Fran	licks	
	get	nips	
	glad	pick	
	Jack	pup	
	jumps	pups	

PIG'S TRIP	Decodable Words		High-Frequency Words
	gets	packs	a
	gift	picks	for
	helps	pig	gives
	him	six	on
	his	tricks	
	jet	trip	
	Kim	up	
	kiss	wig	
	mitt		

RICK'S DESK	Decodable Words	
	box	not
	clips	pens
	cup	quick
	desk	Rick
	fits	scrubs
	fix	stamps
	mess	ten

The word list shows where each word first appears.

MAX GETS HIS WISH

Decodable Words

bath	sit
deck	that's
fish	will
jog	wish
rod	
ship	

CAT AND HIS PALS

Decodable Words

		High-Frequency Word
bees	path	give
cab	see	
dash	sees	
duck	sip	
got	three	
pals		

PUP AND BUG

Decodable Words

bug	mug
bun	red
dish	rug
luck	top
mat	tub

BUD HAS SIX PUPS

Decodable Words

		High-Frequency Words
beds	jump	out
Bud	lot	ride
dig	mud	small
dog	that	
go	tuck	
he	tucks	
hop	wet	

The word list shows where each word first appears.

DOT IN POP'S SHOP

Decodable Words

be	pot
dolls	rocks
dot	shop
hops	sits
jug	slips
lots	sock
naps	wigs
Pop's	

BOB BUG

Decodable Words | | **High-Frequency Words**

am	quacked	are
Bob	sad	I
Buglet	sat	said
Don	sobbed	you
felt	then	
met	yes	
pal		

WET PETS

Decodable Words | | **High-Frequency Word**

Ben	pen	wants
grass	pets	
help	shed	
hen	them	
lets	yet	
pecks		

IN THE HOT SUN

Decodable Words

hat	pads
look	Seth
mom	she

The word list shows where each word first appears.

200

LET'S GO SEE BUGS

Decodable Words		High-Frequency Words
as	looked	good
book	math	put
bugs	Miss	
bus	Nell	
dogs	pigs	
frogs	thin	
had	took	
jar	we	
Jill	wings	
kids	yelled	

BEE AND DUCK

Decodable Words		High-Frequency Word
back	lost	her
bee	quack	
but	rock	
buzz	sack	
cash	sick	
frog	so	
lands	still	

BANG, THUMP, PING!

Decodable Words		High-Frequency Words
asked	ping	could
band	skunk	what
bang	sniff	
best	stand	
did	tall	
flag	thing	
it's	thump	
land	went	
napped		

The word list shows where each word first appears.

I Would if I Could	**Decodable Words**		**High-Frequency Word**
	bat	much	saw
	branch	off	
	called	past	
	can't	pond	
	cubs	ran	
	flap	splash	
	fox	us	

The Twin's Tricks	**Decodable Words**		**High-Frequency Words**
	all	gong	down
	blasted	grabbed	was
	Brad	handstands	
	brass	held	
	clanged	himself	
	clapped	jumped	
	class	landed	
	dressed	legs	
	dropped	planned	
	drum	plop	
	drummed	stunt	
	flip	triple	
	flipped	trumpet	
	flips	trusted	
	flop	twin	
	flung	twins	
	gasped	twist	
	Glen		

The word list shows where each word first appears.

JILL AND CLIFF'S PUMPKINS

Decodable Words		High-Frequency Words
an	pits	any
bottle	plants	from
brim	plump	grow
Cliff	prints	new
clumps	pumpkin	old
crop	pumpkins	
crush	sticks	
digs	tags	
drops	tend	
fall	trickles	
fills	twists	
milk	until	
next		

CHET CHICK

Decodable Words	
brand	lunch
champ	munched
checked	nest
Chet	rubbed
chick	such
chin	thanks
flapped	think
inch	when
just	winked

The word list shows where each word first appears.

LUNCH KIT

Decodable Words		High-Frequency Word
added	let	do
apples	lunches	
bell	mixed	
blank	must	
bunch	nuts	
Chad	pan	
chopped	pink	
chunks	rang	
cook	sink	
cooked	smelled	
drink	tenth	
eggs	tree	
fixed	trunk	
flat	whip	
ham	whipped	
handed	whisk	
isn't	wink	
kit		

The word list shows where each word first appears.

JAKE'S RAKE

Decodable Words		High-Frequency Word
brave	puffed	want
chase	rake	
game	raked	
games	raking	
gave	save	
gazed	scales	
hands	shape	
hate	snake	
hissed	snakes	
huffed	spot	
hugs	stuffed	
Jake	stuffing	
Jane	tag	
little	trade	
made	trash	
mistake	waved	
names	wiggled	
no		

The word list shows where each word first appears.

KATE'S CAKE

Decodable Words		High-Frequency Words
ate	late	know
baked	mix	one
branches	name	where
cake	plate	why
came	pots	
chimp	same	
Dave	scribbled	
didn't	shade	
fake	shopping	
giggled	take	
glass		
gulp		
Kate		

The word list shows where each word first appears.